(Canada)

Discord

Map Legend

- ⚔ battlefields
- ⚑ forts
- ⛏ goldfields

State borders reflect today's boundaries.

Fort Buford

BATTLE OF KILLDEER MOUNTAIN

Little Missouri River

Fort Lincoln

Fort Rice

Fort Yates

NORTH DAKOTA

STANDING ROCK INDIAN RESERVATION

Grand River

STANDING ROCK AGENCY

MINNESOTA

GREAT SIOUX RESERVATION

BLACK HILLS

(Paha Sapa)

Cheyenne River

Fort Pierre

SOUTH DAKOTA

White River

Missouri River

PINE RIDGE INDIAN RESERVATION

BATTLE OF WOUNDED KNEE

Fort Randall

IOWA

Fort Robinson

Niobrara River

North Platte River

GREAT PLAINS

NEBRASKA

N
W — E
S

RED CLOUD

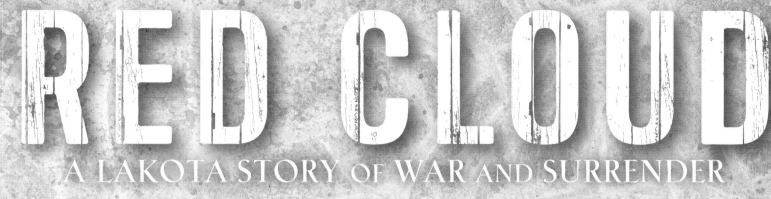

A LAKOTA STORY OF WAR AND SURRENDER

S. D. NELSON

Abrams Books for Young Readers
New York

For the strong-hearted athletes on
the Pine Ridge Reservation—
Ho-ka hey! Lace up your shoes and get in the game.
Now is your time in the sun.

—S. D. Nelson, Mahpíya Kiŋy' Aŋ

I was born a Lakota and I have lived as a Lakota and I shall die a Lakota. —Red Cloud, Makhpiya-luta

My people were battle-hardened warriors. We had to be in order to survive in a world of conflict. As nomadic horsemen who roamed the vast grasslands of America, we wandered freely and hunted the enormous herds of buffalo. They provided us with food, clothing, and the skins for our tipis. Many different Indian tribes lived on the prairies. Our people were known as the Lakota, or Sioux. We were divided into seven smaller tribes. My tribe was called the Oglala.

We seven tribes of Lakota shared the same language and customs. But we were not united under one chief or leader. We did not have, or need, an organized army. Any conflict with an enemy was usually a skirmish or small battle between tribes, never a large-scale war between nations. Fortunately, we had trusted friends and allies: the Cheyenne and the Arapaho.

Indian woman drying meat on a rack before a tipi, Fort Belknap Reservation. Lakota women would have performed similar tasks within their community.

Other tribes were our hated enemies: the Crow, Pawnee, Omaha, Shoshone, and Rees. They were always trying to steal our beloved horses and plunder our villages. In order to overcome them, we had to make ourselves more dangerous than they were. We became the raiders of the Great Plains! We armed ourselves like the Wolf, with his fangs, and the powerful Grizzly, with his claws.

My Lakota people believed that a spirit lives in all things: *Wakan Tanka*, the Great Mystery. Wakan Tanka favored the warrior who was fearless in battle. We believed that such a warrior would surely defeat the enemy—or at least die with honor. Stories would be told remembering the warrior as a hero.

> [It is] our manifest destiny to overspread and to possess the whole of the continent which Providence [God] has given us for the development of the great experiment of liberty. —John L. O'Sullivan, American editor of *New York Morning News*, 1845

Before my birth, my people had struggled against our enemies to establish a homeland for ourselves in the Black Hills. We Lakota called this new land *Paha Sapa* and believed it to be our sacred place on earth. But the ever-changing world was unpredictable. Strange people with pale skin came up the rivers into our country. Because of their white skin, we called them *wasichus*. They brought new, rare treasures—metal knives, colored cloth, glass beads, kettles for cooking, sugar, and other amazing things. Their most desirable trade item, however, was the musket. It sent a burning bolt of lightning with the power to kill! In exchange for these goods, the traders wanted beaver pelts and buffalo hides, which they sold far away in their great villages called cities.

The wasichus built a trading post in the heart of our country. It grew in size and became known as Fort Laramie. Many Indian tribes gathered at the fort to trade with the wasichus. I must admit that I, too, was fascinated by their wondrous gifts, especially the powerful muskets. Fort Laramie was followed by another trading post, and then another. And soon the traders were followed by throngs of wasichus. They came swarming like ants. They built very long roads, which they called the Oregon Trail and the Bozeman Trail. Wagon trains full of people—men, women, and children—traveled through our land, killing the buffalo as they went. They were trespassers and had no business in our country. They did not ask; they blazed through. They claimed they were headed to faraway lands called California and Montana in search of gold—the yellow metal that makes white men crazy.

The wasichus slaughtered buffalo for their hides as well as for sport, greatly diminishing their numbers. Here a man stands atop a pile of buffalo skulls. Native Americans also killed the buffalo in great numbers and exchanged the hides for trade items.

The white men are like locusts when they fly so thick
that the whole sky is a snowstorm . . .
white men with guns in their hands will come faster
than you can count. —Little Crow, Taóyate Dúta

The U.S Army was sent west to protect the settlers as they crossed Lakota lands.

We Lakota refused to be pushed aside by the intruders. Sometimes we used our raiding tactics against the wagon trains and trading posts. Instead of trading buffalo hides, we began to take what we wanted from the trespassing wasichus. We stole their horses and guns, burned their wagons—and took scalps, too.

We soon discovered that the wasichus had an army. From the east, soldiers came to protect their people. We called these soldiers "bluecoats" because of the color of their uniforms. They guarded the trading posts and built forts. It became clear to me and other Lakota that the wasichus planned to devour the land and conquer us.

As the years passed, I honed my fighting instincts and leadership skills. Other Lakota were just as brave in battle, but my decisions often resulted in victory. I remember leading a horse-stealing raid into Shoshone country in the summer of 1849. With twelve men under my command, we traveled west from the Black Hills for many days. The journey was long and tiring before we finally came upon our quarry: a large Shoshone encampment.

Our attack took the enemy completely by surprise, and we drove off with a herd of sixty horses. I led by example, and my men followed. Nonetheless, I was not yet looked upon as a chief. That honor would be bestowed on me later.

> The Great Spirit [Wakan Tanka] raised both the white man and the Indian. I think he raised the Indian first. He raised me in this land and it belongs to me. —Red Cloud, Makhpiya-luta

1851—FIRST FORT LARAMIE TREATY

In the summer of 1851, the United States government requested all the Indian tribes to meet at Fort Laramie for a council. Those invited were friends of the Lakota, such as the Cheyenne, as well as hated enemies, like the Crow. The bluecoats promised us gifts of blankets, sacks of flour, clothing, and the like. More than ten thousand Indians from various tribes answered the call. It was the largest gathering I had ever seen on the prairies! There were thousands of tipis and horse herds that were beyond counting.

The U.S. government wanted our leaders to sign treaty papers that would allow safe passage of their wagon trains through our country. But how were we supposed to respond? The Lakota did not have one leader or a set of chiefs who spoke for all the people. So the bluecoats chose Chief Conquering Bear (Matḣó Wayúhi) to represent the Lakota bands—because he agreed to their terms. He signed the Fort Laramie Treaty of 1851, and others did as well. They wanted the offered gifts. I did not sign.

As soon as the U.S. government representatives left, many Indians returned to their old behavior of intertribal warfare and the raiding of wagon trains. The bluecoats said we broke our treaty with them. But we had not. One chief or warrior could not sign for all the different bands of Lakota. The U.S. government could not comprehend this. It was a free way of living and of governing that was alien to them.

> We hope that the Government will render such aid as will enable the citizens of the north to carry on a war of extermination until the last Redskin of these tribes has been killed. —*Yreka Herald*, August 7, 1853

AUGUST 19, 1854—THE GRATTAN BATTLE/MASSACRE

A few years later, in the heat of summer, more than five hundred tipis stood at the outskirts of Fort Laramie. Thousands of Indians were gathered to receive their treaty goods. However, the rations of food and blankets were not being given as promised. So when a lame cow strayed from a passing wagon train, a hungry Lakota man shot and killed it. Lieutenant John L. Grattan led a force of thirty men out from the fort to arrest the warrior. They were supported by two cannons. Chief Conquering Bear tried to convince the warrior who had killed the cow to surrender, but the man refused. An argument followed. Lieutenant Grattan became impatient and ordered his men to form a skirmish line. A soldier fired into the crowd of onlookers. The air filled with bullets and cannon shot. A withering cloud of arrows followed. The young boy known

The U.S. soldiers used cannons like this mountain howitzer in their attacks on villages.

as Crazy Horse (Tashunka Witco), who would later be a great warrior, was there and saw what happened. Spotted Tail (Siŋté Gleška) was also there and fought fiercely to defend our people.

My men joined the fray, and we finished off Lieutenant Grattan and his bluecoats in short order. Our blood was boiling with anger. We took scalps and slashed the bodies of our enemy. We believed doing this meant that these men would enter the world after this one with ruined bodies, unable to enjoy all that it offered. We took their horses and guns, too. We Indians called what happened a battle, just one of many to save our people. But the wasichus' newspapers called it a massacre, as if the Lakota had provoked it. The wasichus stirred themselves into an uproar that sought revenge against us. Many more battles would follow.

When I was young among our nation, I was poor,
but from wars with one nation and another
I raised myself to be a chief. —Red Cloud, Makhpiya-luta

1855—THE PIPE DANCE

In the summer of 1855, we Oglala Lakota were encamped on the banks of the White River. We had come together to celebrate the Pipe Dance ceremony called the *Hunka*. This ritual proclaimed the names of new tribal chiefs. I was one of a group of men chosen by the elders to be honored that day. We were told that we now carried the burden of responsibility for the welfare of our people. Drumming, dancing, and singing followed. Our confirmation as chiefs was made final by the smoking of the sacred pipe.

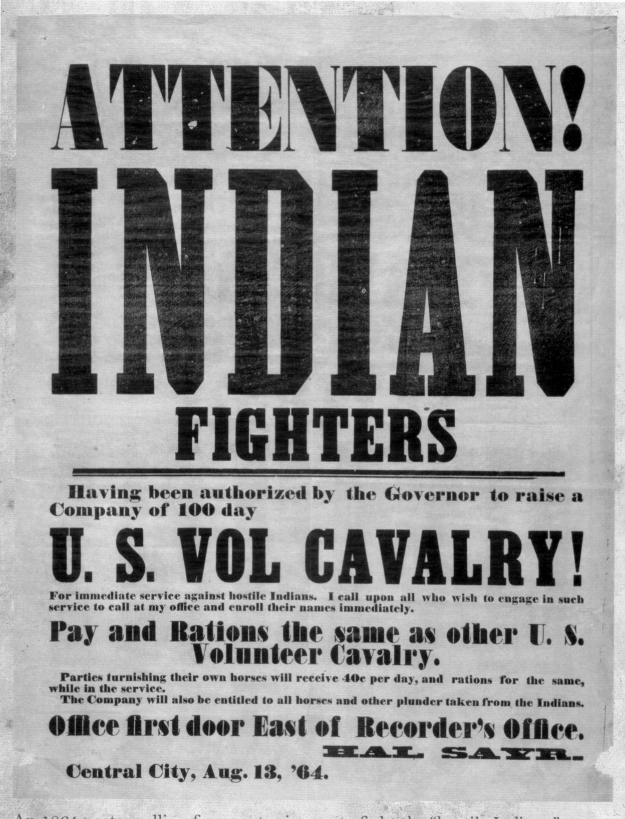

An 1864 poster calling for men to sign up to fight the "hostile Indians."

Kill and scalp all, big and little. Nits make lice.

—Colonel John M. Chivington

NOVEMBER 29, 1864—THE SAND CREEK BATTLE / MASSACRE

Through the following years, the skirmishes between my people and the U.S. government went on. The U.S. government continued to claim that we were breaking the Fort Laramie Treaty. We continued to protect our land and way of life.

With the onset of winter, Colonel John M. Chivington led a force of seven hundred bluecoats against a sleeping Cheyenne village in the wasichu territory of Colorado. Their cannons opened fire at dawn, blasting the tipis apart. The bluecoats gunned down two hundred men, women, and children and mutilated their bodies. Afterward, they went on to Denver in triumph, brandishing the scalps, severed fingers, and other body parts of the slain innocents. The wasichus called the fight a battle; we Indians called it a massacre.

The Cheyenne were our good friends. That terrible slaughter did more to unite us Plains Indians than any other event. Now we had a common enemy. And many people looked to me as their war chief. Different bands from the Lakota, Cheyenne, and Arapaho joined forces with me, although some chose not to. I gave orders for a series of raids on ranches, farms, wagon trains, and trading posts. We would push the intruders out of our country once and for all! During the next several months, we killed more whites than the number of Indians killed by the bluecoats at Sand Creek.

Titon Sioux

Oglala — Red Cloud - Makhpiya Luta
Brule
Minniconju
Sans Arc
Blackfoot
Two Kettles
Hunkpapa — Sitting Bull - Tatanka Iyotake

Our attacks were no longer random but were carefully planned. We used elements of surprise. Instead of forming in organized ranks like the bluecoats, we attacked in small groups on more than one front. I instructed my men to hide in prairie gullies and thickets. Whenever the bluecoats traveled on their roads, they risked losing their lives. Time after time, we caught the enemy unprepared.

> We wanted a much bigger war-party so that we could meet the soldiers and get revenge. But this was hard, because the people were not all of the same mind, and they were hungry and cold. —Black Elk, Heȟáka Sápa

1866—SECOND FORT LARAMIE TREATY

In the spring of 1866, the U.S. government again called for a council meeting of all Indian tribes at Fort Laramie. It wanted to stop Indian raids on wagon trains once and for all. The government sent Colonel B. Henry Carrington to negotiate the treaty. Colonel Carrington arrived with one thousand men. He, too, came with gifts—sacks of sugar, coffee, tobacco, colored cloth, and more. He pretended that his goal was asking the tribes to allow the U.S. government to build a new road and to offer safe passage for all white settlers, miners, and soldiers through our country. In fact, the colonel already had orders to build forts to protect the people traveling through Indian lands on the Bozeman Trail. The treaty was a sham.

Every chief voiced his opinion. Some wanted the offered gifts and said they were willing to sign the U.S. government's treaty papers. Spotted Tail, a Brulé Lakota chief, signed. Leaders of other bands also agreed to put pen to paper and enjoyed their cheap trinkets and gifts of coffee, sugar, and the like. For many, the lure of whiskey was also too great. Those Indians replaced the one true spirit in this life with a liquid spirit, drunk from a bottle.

The United States agrees that for every thirty children between said ages who can be induced or compelled to attend school, a house shall be provided, and a teacher,

FORT C.F. SMITH

MONTANA

WYOMING

FORT PHIL KEARNY

FORT RENO

But as in the past, those leaders who signed did not represent the desire of all our people. I was furious. When my turn to speak came, I stood and told the colonel what I thought of the American president and his gifts: "The Great Father sends us presents and wants a new road. But the White Chief already goes with soldiers to steal the road before the Indian says yes or no. I will talk with you no more. I will go now, and I will fight you. As long as I live I will fight you for the last hunting grounds." My Oglala band struck our tipis, and we left Fort Laramie.

8 March coffee
" 1 bacon
" 2 bags flour
9 March 2 beans
" 2 bacon
" 2 candles
" 1 raisins
" 1 crackers

These Indians [are] the enemies of our race and of our civilization . . . —William Tecumseh Sherman

Colonel Carrington left Fort Laramie, too. He led his army northward to follow his orders to build even more forts along the Bozeman Trail. From such positions of strength, he could offer protection to the wagon trains traveling through our country. My scouts watched the advance of his troops and counted their numbers.

The colonel selected a site on the broad grassland between two streams flowing with fresh water. The land afforded ample pasturage for their livestock and a good vantage point from which to see approaching Indians. Wood for fort con-struction and for fires would be supplied from the forested hills close at hand. So construction began on Fort Phil Kearny.

The log walls were not yet up when I led our first attack, at dawn. We caught them sleeping, and drove off with nearly two hundred mules and horses. Some of the enemy mounted their remaining horses and gave chase. But they seemed to have no fighting plan. We turned on them, killing several. Our blood was up! With angry hearts, we scalped them and cut off their arms and legs so they would be dismembered in the world after this one.

Whenever the soldiers left their fort to cut trees for construction or to gather firewood, my scouts were watching. They regularly reported to me about the comings and goings at Fort Phil Kearny. As soon as the wasichus' wagons ventured far from the protection of their fort, we would attack. Autumn came, and winter followed. We continued to harass the enemy.

Our old way of wildly attacking enemy tribes like the Crow did not work against the firepower of the bluecoats. Before, we fought as individuals seeking personal glory. Now, as war chief, I made plans and gave orders so that we would fight as a team. I organized my men into fighting units that would attack outposts and wagon trains that were miles apart at the same time. With great success, my warriors stopped and turned back the trespassers. The U.S. Army called the many battles between our peoples Red Cloud's War.

FORT LARAMIE IDH. T.

A contemporary drawing of Fort Laramie. "IDH. T." stands for "Idaho Territory."

The riches that we have in this world . . . we cannot take with us to the next world. I wish to know why the Commissioners are sent out to us who do nothing but rob us and get the riches of this world away from us?

—Red Cloud, Makhpiya-luta

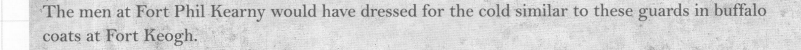

The men at Fort Phil Kearny would have dressed for the cold similar to these guards in buffalo coats at Fort Keogh.

DECEMBER 21, 1866—THE FETTERMAN BATTLE / MASSACRE

I made plans to set a trap for Colonel Carrington's men. I prayed to Wakan Tanka to keep my people strong.

Snow lay in the valleys of the rolling prairie. It was in one such valley, among the thickets and scrub brush, that my Lakota, Cheyenne, and Arapaho men hid—two thousand strong. I had taught them a new way of fighting—to hold back their horses, control their eagerness to win personal glory, and await the order to attack as one force.

Morning dawned, and the usual woodcutting wagons left Fort Phil Kearny, accompanied by ninety armed men. I had a small group of warriors go out to harass them. In response, Colonel Carrington sent a reinforcement of eighty bluecoats from his fort, under the command of Captain William J. Fetterman. The captain had proven himself to be a fearless leader during his country's brutal Civil War. His orders were to rescue the woodcutters but not pursue the Indians. Captain Fetterman drove off my small raiding party. The fight could have ended as a brief skirmish, like so many before. But that was not my plan.

Ho-ka hey! It is a good day to fight! It is a good day to die! Strong hearts, brave hearts, to the front!

—Crazy Horse, Tashunka Witco

I sent my Oglala warrior Crazy Horse and a few others to act as a decoy. They taunted Captain Fetterman. Then, alone, Crazy Horse rode back and forth on a nearby hillside, provoking the captain. The army officer took the bait. He led his men in pursuit of Crazy Horse over the rolling prairie—directly toward my waiting warriors.

What followed would be called a massacre by some; all would agree it was a terrible battle. As Captain Fetterman's men descended the hill into the valley, my two thousand warriors emerged from hiding. The soldiers carried rifles and six-shooter revolvers. My men were armed mostly with bows, arrows, and tomahawks.

Volleys of gunfire exploded with a roar. Thousands of arrows filled the air. The fighting soon became hand to hand, with pistols, clubs, and knives. Many of my men gave their lives. When we finished, all eighty-one bluecoats lay dead. We took their weapons, we took their scalps, and we disfigured their bodies.

In order to insure the civilization of the Indians entering into this treaty the necessity of Education is admitted, especially by such of them as are or may be settled on said agricultural reservations, and they therefore pledge themselves to compel their children, male and female, between the ages of six and sixteen years, to attend school, and it is hereby made the duty of the Agent for said Indians, to see that this stipulation is strictly complied with.

We had stopped these intruders with our might. My people were thrilled with our victory. The U.S. government was stunned. It was forced to reevaluate its plan to simply push us aside. In 1867, its Congress created the Indian Peace Commission. Its purpose was to end hostilities with the Indians so the white man's advancement on the continent could continue without conflict. The idea was that the U.S. government would give our people land called reservations. We would have to give up our free-roaming, hunting ways and learn to become farmers. The U.S. Army would enforce the new plan with foot soldiers and cavalry. They would be armed with terrible firepower—breech-loading rifles and cannons that fired exploding shells.

In August 1867, President Grant appointed Phil Sheridan (*far left*) to head the Division of the Missouri (under the direction of the War Department) and to pacify the Plains. George Armstrong Custer (*far right*) was the man responsible for the terrible disaster that befell him and his men at the Battle of the Little Bighorn.

All Indians not on reservations are hostile and will remain so until killed off.

—William Tecumseh Sherman

A warrior fights to protect his people. So we continued our attacks against the other forts and wagon trains along the Bozeman Trail. It was one battle after another. But we were outnumbered and outgunned by the U.S. Army. The winters were especially cruel, for there were not enough buffalo left to feed and clothe my people.

There comes a time when a chief must admit that the enemy is too powerful, that to keep fighting will only end with the complete destruction of everything he loves. It was clear to me as war chief that we could not continue. Doing so meant only ruin for our children. There was no other way out. It was time to surrender and accept the rations of food and clothing offered by the U.S. government.

Chief Spotted Tail
(Siŋté Gleška)

Chief Conquering Bear
(Matȟó Wayúhi)

Chief Sitting Bull
(Ťhatȟáŋka Íyotake)

Colonel John M.
Chivington

Captain William J.
Fetterman

Colonel Henry B.
Carrington

We must think of the women and children and that it is very bad for them. So we must make peace.

—Red Cloud, Makhpiya-luta

Indian chiefs in council with General Sherman and commissioners at Fort Laramie.

Titon Siou

Ogla
Brule
Minn
Sans
Blackfoot
Two Kettles
Hunkpapa   — Sitting Bull - Tatanka Iyotake

1868—THIRD FORT LARAMIE TREATY

Nevertheless, it was our many victories that forced the U.S. government to negotiate a new treaty—the Fort Laramie Treaty of 1868. The peace commissioners agreed to close the Bozeman Trail and the three forts that guarded it. Only Fort Laramie would remain nearby. They promised to stop attacking my people if we moved and settled on the land they called the Great Sioux Reservation. We would be given food and taught the new ways of civilization. Best of all, we would be given the sacred Black Hills and the surrounding prairies with their enormous hunting grounds. We had won the war against the U.S. government, the long fight that they had called Red Cloud's War!

Government agents with sacks of food rations to be distributed at the Great Sioux Reservation.

I was no longer chief. The war was over. For the sake of my own people, those who followed me, I accepted and signed the new treaty papers. But of course I did not represent the desire of all the people. Opinions were divided—leaders like Sitting Bull (Tȟatȟáŋka Íyotake) and Crazy Horse questioned my leadership and rejected the treaty, like the ones before it. They would continue to fight, along with their many followers, jeopardizing our new peace treaty. But other chiefs, like Spotted Tail, agreed and signed. Then I sent my men to burn the abandoned forts to the ground. After that, with mixed feelings of relief and shame, my people moved onto the reservation.

I knew that I did not speak for all the Plains Indian tribes. There were holdouts who still wanted our old Indian ways of freedom. They did not yet understand that the flood of wasichus was unstoppable. Some Lakota leaders, like Sitting Bull and Crazy Horse, even called me a traitor. They refused to accept the obvious need to surrender. The whites called them "hostiles." Many Indian people followed them. But as I foresaw, terrible battles followed.

> [Red Cloud is] undoubtedly the most celebrated warrior now living on the American Continent . . . a good ruler, an eloquent speaker, an able general and fair diplomat. —*New York Times*, June 1, 1870

In 1870 I traveled east with a small group of Indians to meet with the president of the United States, Ulysses S. Grant. I felt like a lowly dog, but I held my head high. We traveled on an iron horse—called a train—with a roaring fire burning in its belly. As we traveled, I was stunned to see bridges that spanned wide rivers, endless roads that connected city after city, and tall buildings standing like man-made hills with glass windows glowing in the night.

In Washington, D.C., crowds gathered by the thousands to see us. President Grant spoke to me with respect as his equal. But we both knew that I was the defeated commander. Yes, I held my head high. But inside, I felt like a boy thrown hard from his horse. The power of the wasichus was beyond question. Truly, they were a fearsome warrior people!

Thousands of armed bluecoats marched across parade grounds with their flags flying. I was taken to a place called a harbor, where ships of war traveled on the great ocean to faraway lands. The shores of the wasichus' kingdom were armed with cannons as big as trees that hurled huge exploding bombs. It seemed certain that anyone who dared to challenge them would be met with utter destruction.

Waterfront of U.S. Navy Yard, Washington, D.C.

The Red Cloud delegation to the east coast (*Red Cloud, seated, in center*).

My lodges were many, but now they are few. The White Man wants all. —Red Cloud, Makhpiya-luta

In the end, the U.S. government once again did not honor the treaty that we signed for our people. The wasichus found gold in the Black Hills and took the sacred land from us by force. They divided the Great Sioux Reservation into smaller tracts of land. The Indians called "hostiles" did not keep the Lakota part of the treaty, either—but they had not signed it. Many battles followed. The Lakota chiefs Sitting Bull and Crazy Horse gave their lives resisting. Stories are still told of how they died—as warrior heroes!

I did not die as a warrior hero in glorious battle. I am remembered as the one who signed the treaty papers and surrendered.

My hair has turned white . . . like the snows of winter setting in hard upon me. Still, it is proper for an old man to remember the stories of his youth . . . So I speak of warm spring days when we boys rode our painted horses bareback across the prairies, howling like coyotes with the wind in our hair.

Home of Chief Red Cloud at the Pine Ridge Agency (*people unidentified*).

But remember this: The story of my people is not finished. It goes on. The flame of hope still burns in our hearts. We remain warriors, for living in this world requires strong hearts. We are not injured victims of the past. I have no stomach for that. I believe in the future of my Lakota people. The best part of our story is ours for the telling and the doing . . .

SELECT TIME LINE

1778: Treaty of Fort Pitt. The first treaty agreed to between a Native American nation (the Lenni Lenape, called the Delaware by whites) and the new United States. By establishing the "treaty process," the two parties recognize each other's sovereign nature and their right to exist as nations. Many treaties between Indian nations and the United States will follow.

1821: Red Cloud is born along Blue Creek, which flows into the North Platte River in present-day Nebraska.

1836: The Oregon Trail is established as the primary route for wagon trains heading west.

1837–38: Red Cloud is sixteen years old when he rides in his first war party against the Pawnee.

1845: John L. O'Sullivan, editor of *New York Morning News*, declares that it is "our manifest destiny to overspread the [North American] continent allotted by Providence [God] for the free development of our yearly multiplying millions."

1848: Gold is discovered in California. Thousands of emigrants pass through Lakota hunting grounds.

1848–50: Red Cloud marries Pretty Owl, and they have the first of their six children (five daughters and a son).

1851: The Fort Laramie Treaty is signed by individual chiefs without the authority to speak for all Native American peoples. The U.S. government tries to placate the Indians with gifts and annuities in order to allow safe passage of emigrants accross the Great Plains. Red Cloud (not yet a confirmed leader/chief) attends.

1854 (August 19): The Grattan Battle. A Lakota man kills a stray cow belonging to a member of an emigrant wagon train. Lieutenant John L. Grattan, known to be a hard-drinking man, confronts the Miniconjou Lakota chief, Conquering Bear. The chief offers to make full payment for the dead cow. But Lieutenant Grattan insists on arresting the man who killed the cow. A fierce fight follows. Many Lakota are killed. Lieutenant Grattan and all his men are killed. The American press declares the fight a "massacre." Red Cloud takes part and probably kills his first white man.

1855: Battle of Blue Water (also known as the Battle/Massacre of Ash Creek). The U.S. Army retaliates against the Lakota by attacking a Brulé Lakota village. Cannons blast the village with grapeshot, killing eighty-six Lakota men, women, and children.

1855: Pipe Dance ceremony confirms Red Cloud as a headman, or chief. He is thirty-four years old.

1862: Gold is discovered in Montana.

1863: John Bozeman leads the first wagon train into the Powder River country, headed for the goldfields of western Montana. He is turned back by Lakota and Cheyenne. But he is persistent and returns to establish the Bozeman Trail. Thousands of emigrants will follow this route through Lakota territory.

1864 (November 29): The Sand Creek Battle/Massacre: At dawn, Colonel John M. Chivington leads seven hundred U.S. Army volunteers in an attack against the sleeping Cheyenne in Chief Black Kettle's village. The soldiers kill, scalp, and mutilate approximately two hundred men, women, and children.

1865–66: The U.S. Army builds three forts along the Bozeman Trail from which it can provide forces to protect the influx of wagon trains traveling through Indian country.

1866 (December 21): The Fetterman Battle/Massacre: Red Cloud orders his warriors to lure Captain William J. Fetterman and his men into a trap. Led by Crazy Horse, the attacking Lakota and Cheyenne kill all eighty-one soldiers.

1866–68: Red Cloud's War with the U.S. Army, consisting of countless raids on wagon trains, essentially halts the flow of traffic. The U.S. government recognizes Red Cloud to be the head chief of the Lakota Sioux.

1868 (April 29): Red Cloud and other Indian leaders sign a new Fort Laramie Treaty. The agreement creates the Great Sioux Reservation, which includes all of western present-day South Dakota (including Paha Sapa, the Black Hills). In return, the U.S. government closes the Bozeman Trail and the three forts that protect it. In addition, it promises to provide rations and clothing for thirty years. Sitting Bull and Crazy Horse continue to lead fierce resistance.

1874: Gold is discovered in the Black Hills.

1876 (October 24): General George Crook deposes Red Cloud and appoints the more conciliatory Spotted Tail as head chief and negotiator for the Lakota Sioux.

1877: Congress reneges on the 1868 Fort Laramie Treaty and signs into law an appropriation bill (technically not a treaty) that confiscates the Black Hills and eliminates Indian rights to the hunting grounds in the Bighorn River basin. Red Cloud and other chiefs sign the agreement under threat of not receiving rations and being forced to move their people to Indian Territory in present-day Oklahoma.

1878 (October): Red Cloud settles at the Pine Ridge Agency in South Dakota.

1909 (December 10): Red Cloud, who had been baptized and had accepted the Catholic religion, dies and is buried the following day. He sleeps beneath the prairie grass on the hill above Red Cloud Indian School, on the Pine Ridge Indian Reservation in South Dakota.

AUTHOR'S NOTE

Red Cloud's War stopped the advance of the U.S. Army onto the Great Plains.

Under Red Cloud's leadership and coordinated resistance, the Lakota, Cheyenne, and Arapaho forced the U.S. government to seek a peace settlement. Outnumbered and outgunned by this mighty industrialized foe, Chief Red Cloud believed he had little choice; to continue fighting would only end in defeat. He signed the Fort Laramie Treaty of 1868. Under the agreement, the entire western half of present-day South Dakota, including the Black Hills, would have remained "Indian Country."

The fractious nature of the free-roaming tribes had always hindered any hope of an enduring unity, especially against common enemies. The Lakota chiefs Red Cloud, Sitting Bull, and Crazy Horse were in constant competition with one another, trying to achieve the highest status as warrior chiefs. In the end they developed an intense rivalry. Whereas Red Cloud signed the treaty, other chiefs like Sitting Bull and Crazy Horse refused agreement and compromise, and they did not sign. Along with their followers, they kept fighting. Eventually the U.S. Army crushed them. The government took back the Black Hills and much of the land previously allotted to the Indians.

Kevin Gover (Pawnee), the director of the National Museum of the American Indian, Smithsonian, says, "Treaties rest at the heart of Native American history as well as contemporary tribal life and identity. The approximately 368 treaties that were negotiated and signed by U.S. commissioners and tribal leaders . . . enshrine promises our government made to Indian Nations." The treaty-making process inherently acknowledges the "nation" status of both Native American tribes and the American government. Legal arguments for the implementation and final settlement of the treaties are ongoing. Many Native Americans and historians question the government's intentions and the resulting outcome of treaties. James Riding (Pawnee) has said that "the U.S. government, driven by imperialistic impulses and a sense of racial superiority, used treaties and policy making as implements of social control, political domination, and cultural genocide."

Life on Indian reservations today has been described as living in a Third World country or a prison without walls. A 2014 article by Sari Horwitz in the *Washington Post* described the depressed situation in the following way: "A toxic collection of pathologies—poverty, unemployment, domestic violence, sexual assault, alcoholism and drug addiction—has seeped into the lives of young people among the nation's 566 tribes. Reversing their crushing hopelessness, Indian experts say, is one of the biggest challenges for these communities."

This sobering assessment of reservation life is not what Chief Red Cloud and others intended when they signed the offered treaty papers nearly 150 years ago. Perhaps some government officials (who are long since dead) would not have wished such a fate upon future generations, either. While blame can be placed, it offers no solution. Red Cloud's intention in agreeing to sign the treaty was an *impossible dream*. He hoped that his people would be able to carry on their free-roaming way of life. They would possess an immense area of land (i.e., the Great Sioux Reservation), where they could always hunt buffalo. Red Cloud imagined the only contact with the wasichus would be at trading posts beyond their reservation borders, where the Indians could still acquire coffee, sugar, guns, and other desired objects. And of course, they would continue to obtain horses through trade and by raiding the Crow and other enemy tribes. The Fort Laramie Treaty of 1868 stated that the U.S. government would provide subsidies for the welfare of the Native people. It did not, and it failed American Indians in other ways. After all these years a collective resentment remains. Many Native Americans feel that the U.S. government is an immoral perpetrator and that they live in a state of never-ending victimhood.

Today Indian nations are sovereign countries that govern themselves with self-determination. Like all human beings, Native Americans face the many challenges of a complicated, ever-changing world. Many practice traditions that still serve the people and share them with those who seek understanding. Ancient Lakota ceremonies like the *Inipi* (sweat lodge) and the *Hanbleceya* (vision quest) offer lessons for a steady course of action to a new generation. They provide a way of beauty and of strength—the way of the warrior. Living in the present and reaching for the future requires courage and cooper-

ation. Courage comes to those who seek it. Cooperation is found upon the same path. If we listen, we will find meaning in the words of our Lakota teacher, who, as a boy, had a great vision . . .

"And I saw the sacred hoop of my people was one of many hoops that made one circle; wide as daylight and as starlight, and in the center grew one mighty flowering tree to shelter all the children of one mother and one father. And I saw that it was holy."

—Black Elk, Heȟáka Sápa

ENDNOTES

Note: Section head quotations are not chronological but are relevant and reflective of the time.

page 4: "I was born . . .": Paul, *Autobiography of Red Cloud*, xviii.

page 9: "[It is] our manifest destiny . . .": Editors of Time-Life Books, *War for the Plains*, 20.

page 10: Fort Laramie was followed . . . white men crazy: Larson, *Red Cloud*, 53.

page 12: "The white men . . .": Drury and Clavin, *The Heart of Everything That Is*, 160.

page 15: Our attack . . . sixty horses: Paul, *Autobiography of Red Cloud*, 60–61.

page 17: "The Great Spirit . . .": Drury and Clavin, *The Heart of Everything That Is*, 197.

page 17: One chief or warrior . . . too alien to them: Drury and Clavin, *The Heart of Everything That Is*, 3–4 .

page 18: "We hope that the Government . . .": Geoffrey Ward, *The West*, episode 3, "Speck of the Future," http://www.pbs.org/weta/thewest/program/episodes/three/diggers.htm.

page 18: So when a lame cow . . . : Drury and Clavin, *The Heart of Everything That Is*, 125–30.

page 21: "When I was young . . .": Paul, *Autobiography of Red Cloud*, 24.

page 21: In the summer of 1855, . . . sacred pipe: Paul, *Autobiography of Red Cloud*, 106–11; Drury and Clavin, *The Heart of Everything That Is*, 131–34.

page 23: "Kill and scalp all . . .": Marrin, *Tatan'ka Iyota'ke, Sitting Bull and His World*, 74.

page 23: Afterward, they went on to Denver . . . : Ambrose, *Crazy Horse and Custer*, 151.

page 23: The wasichus called the fight . . . : McDermott, *Red Cloud*, 26.

page 26: "We wanted a much bigger war-party . . .": Neihardt, *Black Elk Speaks*, 269.

page 26: He, too, came with gifts . . . : Drury and Clavin, *The Heart of Everything That Is*, 244–45.

page 26: Spotted Tail . . . : Larson, *Red Cloud*, 116.

page 28: "The Great Father sends . . .": Drury and Clavin, *The Heart of Everything That Is*, 244–45.

page 31: "These Indians . . .": Ward, *The West*, 250.

page 34: "The riches that we have . . .": Ward, *The West*, 239.

page 36: "Ho-ka hey! . . .": Ambrose, *Crazy Horse and Custer*, 435.

page 36: I sent . . . toward my waiting warriors: Drury and Clavin, *The Heart of Everything That Is*, 328–29.

page 38: In 1867, . . . exploding shells: Larson, *Red Cloud*, 106–7, 111; Drury and Clavin, *The Heart of Everything That Is*, 354.

page 40: "All Indians . . .": http://www.pbs.org/weta/the west/people/s_z/sherman.htm

page 42: "We must think . . .": Neihardt, *Black Elk Speaks*, 269.

page 44: For the sake of my own people, . . . moved onto the reservation: Larson, *Red Cloud*, 124.

page 45: The whites called them . . . terrible battles followed: Welch, *Killing Custer, The Battle of the Little Bighorn and the Fate of the Plains Indians.*, 75.

page 46: "[Red Cloud is] . . .": Larson, *Red Cloud*, 129.

page 48: "My lodges were many . . .": Drury and Clavin, *The Heart of Everything That Is*, 4.

page 52: "Treaties rest . . .": PBS *NewsHour*, Sept. 18, 2014

page 52: The government took back: Drury and Clavin, *The Heart of Everything That Is*, 210.

page 52: "the U.S. government . . .": Harjo, *Nation to Nation*, xxii.

page 52: "A toxic collection . . .": Horowitz, *Washington Post*, March 9, 2014.

page 53: Many Native Americans feel: Larson, *Red Cloud*, 118.

page 53: "And I saw . . .": Neihardt, *Black Elk Speaks*, 43.

SELECT BIBLIOGRAPHY

Ambrose, Stephen E. *Crazy Horse and Custer: The Parallel Lives of Two American Warriors.* New York: Doubleday, 1975.

Barnes, Jeff. *Forts of the Northern Plains: Guide to Historic Military Posts of the Plains Indian Wars.* Mechanicsburg, PA: Stackpole Books, 2008.

Berlo, Janet Catherine. *Plains Indian Drawings, 1865–1935.* New York: Harry N. Abrams, 1996.

Capps, Benjamin. *The Indians.* New York: Time-Life Books, 1973.

Catlin, George. *Letters and Notes on the North American Indians.* North Dighton, MA: JG Press, 1995.

Colton, G. W. *Dakota and Wyoming.* Archival map. New York: G. W. and C. B. Colton, 1868.

Drury, Bob, and Tom Clavin. *The Heart of Everything That Is: The Untold Story of Red Cloud, an American Legend.* New York: Simon & Schuster, 2013.

Editors of Time-Life Books. *War for the Plains.* Alexandria, VA: Time-Life Books, 1994.

Harjo, Suzan Shown, ed. *Nation to Nation: Treaties Between the United States and American Indian Nations.* Washington, D.C., and New York: National Museum of the American Indian in association with Smithsonian Books, 2014.

Heim, Joe. "Pamunkey Indians Granted Federal Recognition." *Washington Post*, July 3, 2015.

Hoover, Herbert T., John E. Miller, et al. *A New South Dakota History.* Edited by Harry F. Thompson. Sioux Falls, SD: Center for Western Studies, 2005.

Horwitz, Sari. "The Hard Lives—and High Suicide Rate—of Native American Children on Reservations." *Washington Post*, March 9, 2014.

Larson, Robert W. *Red Cloud: Warrior-Statesman of the Lakota Sioux.* The Oklahoma Western Biographies 13. Norman, OK: University of Oklahoma Press, 1997.

Marrin, Albert. *Tatan'ka Iyota'ke, Sitting Bull and His World.* New York: Dutton Children's Books, 2000.

Marshall, Joseph M. *The Lakota Way: Stories and Lessons for Living.* New York: Viking Compass, 2001.

McDermott, John D. *Red Cloud: Oglala Legend.* Pierre, SD: South Dakota State Historical Society Press, 2015.

Neihardt, John G. *Black Elk Speaks: Being the Life Story of a Holy Man of the Oglala Sioux.* Lincoln, NE: University of Nebraska Press, 1932.

Paul, R. Eli, ed. *Autobiography of Red Cloud: War Leader of the Oglalas.* Helena, MT: Montana Historical Society Press, 1997.

Taylor, Colin F. *The Plains Indians: A Cultural and Historical View of the North American Plains Tribes of the Pre-Reservation Period.* Avenel, NJ: Crescent Books, 1994.

Tillett, Leslie. *Wind on the Buffalo Grass: The Indians' Own Account of the Battle at the Little Big Horn River & the Death of Their Life on the Plains.* New York: Crowell, 1976.

Ward, Geoffrey C. *The West: An Illustrated History.* New York: Little, Brown, 1996.

Welch, James, Stekler, Paul. *Killing Custer, The Battle of the Little Bighorn and the Fate of the Plains Indians.* New York: Penguin Books, 1995.

ACKNOWLEDGMENTS

I must offer heartfelt thanks to my editor at Abrams Books, Howard Reeves. His passionate desire to publish books that give voice to Native American stories ensures that the unique culture of my people will be honored and that diversity will gain greater acceptance. I am also grateful to my friend Dakota Goodhouse, Ozúye Núŋpa (Two Wars), at United Tribes Technical College in Bismarck, North Dakota, for providing the Lakota translation of Indian names.

The illustrations for this book were created with ink, watercolor, and colored pencil on 140 lb. paper, digitally placed on ledger paper. This process was done digitally to ensure readability.

Library of Congress Cataloging-in-Publication Data

Names: Nelson, S. D., author.

Title: Red Cloud : a Lakota story of war and surrender / by S.D. Nelson.

Other titles: Lakota story of war and surrender

Description: New York : Abrams Books for Young Readers, [2017]

Identifiers: LCCN 2016048744 | ISBN 9781419723131

Subjects: LCSH: Red Cloud, 1822-1909—Juvenile literature. | Oglala Indians—Kings and rulers—Biography—Juvenile literature. | Lakota Indians—History—Juvenile literature. | Red Cloud's War, 1866-1867—Juvenile literature.

Classification: LCC E99.O3 N47 2017 | DDC 978.004/9752440092 [B]—dc23

LC record available at https://lccn.loc.gov/2016048744

Text and illustrations copyright © 2017 S. D. Nelson

Book design by Maria T. Middleton

Printed and bound in China

10 9 8 7 6 5 4 3 2 1

Abrams Books for Young Readers are available at special discounts when purchased in quantity for premiums and promotions as well as fundraising or educational use. Special editions can also be created to specification. For details, contact specialsales@abramsbooks.com or the address below.

ABRAMS The Art of Books
115 West 18th Street, New York, NY 10011
abramsbooks.com

IMAGE CREDITS

Cover and title page: Red Cloud. Photographer unknown, Library of Congress: LC-USZ62-91032. **Page 5:** Image Courtesy of Milwaukee Public Museum, #112055. **Page 11:** Wikimedia Commons. **Page 13:** National Archives 777-HQ-264-854. **Page 19:** Photograph by S. D. Nelson. **Page 22:** History Colorado, scan #10035345. **Page 32:** Fort Phil Kearney, American Heritage Center, University of Wyoming. **Page 35:** Ft. Keogh Mount guard mount in buffalo coats, Montana Historical Society Research Center, Archives, #981-359. **Page 39:** National Archives, 111-B-4162. **Page 41** (*clockwise from top left*): Spotted Tail: Photographer unknown, Library of Congress: LC-USZ62-117419. Conquering Bear: Denver Public Library, Western History Collection, X-31522. Photo by Frank A. Rinehart. Sitting Bull: Denver Public Library, Western History Collection, B-67. Photo by D. F. Barry. Col. Henry Carrington: photographer unknown, Library of Congress: LC-B813-6331 B. William Judd Fetterman: Indians-Battles-Fetterman Massacre, American Heritage Center, University of Wyoming. John Chivington: History Colorado, scan #10047783. **Page 42:** National Archives, 111-SC-95986. **Page 43:** SPC BAE 4605 01600804, National Anthropological Archives, Smithsonian Institution. **Page 46:** Wikimedia Commons. **Page 47:** Red Cloud Delegation. Denver Public Library, Western History Collection, Z-2298. Photographer unknown. **Page 48:** Photograph by W. R. Cross, Library of Congress: LC-USZ62-124293.

INDEX

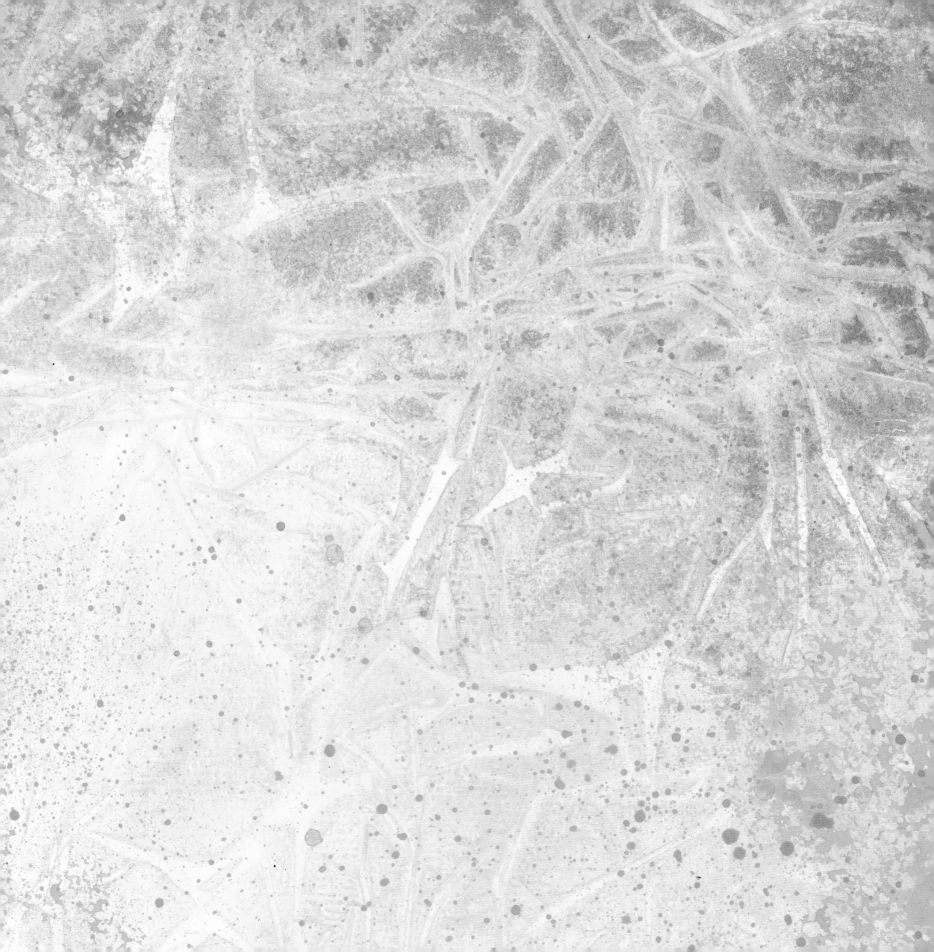